Creating Rapport

Using Personal Power to Influence Without Control

Revised Edition

Elaina Zuker

A Crisp Fifty-Minute™ Series Book

This Fifty-Minute™ Book is designed to be "read with a pencil." It is an excellent workbook for self-study as well as classroom learning. All material is copyright-protected and cannot be duplicated without permission from the publisher. *Therefore, be sure to order a copy for every training participant by contacting:*

1-800-442-7477 ◆ 25 Thomson Place, Boston, MA ◆ www.courseilt.com

Creating Rapport

Using Personal Power to Influence Without Control

Revised Edition

Elaina Zuker

CREDITS:

Senior Editor:	**Debbie Woodbury**
Editor:	**Ann Gosch**
Assistant Editor:	**Genevieve McDermott**
Production Manager:	**Denise Powers**
Design:	**Nicole Phillips**
Production Artist:	**Rich Lehl**

For more information contact:

Course Technology
25 Thomson Place
Boston, MA 02210

Or find us on the Web at **www.courseilt.com**

For permission to use material from this text or product, submit a request online at: www.thomsonrights.com

Any additional questions about permissions can be submitted by e-mail to: thomsonrights@thomson.com

Trademarks

Crisp Fifty-Minute Series is a trademark of Course Technology.

Some of the product names and company names used in this book have been used for identification purposes only and may be trademarks or registered trademarks of their respective manufacturers and sellers.

Disclaimer

Course Technology reserves the right to revise this publication and make changes from time to time in its content without notice.

ISBN 1-4188-4688-0

Library of Congress Catalog Card Number 2005922992

Printed in Canada by Transcontinental Printing

1 2 3 4 5 PM 06 05 04 03

Learning Objectives for

CREATING RAPPORT

The learning objectives for *Creating Rapport* are listed below. They have been developed to guide the user to the core issues covered in this book.

The objectives of this book are to help the user:

1) Understand what is meant by rapport
2) Explore trends in business that call for rapport skills
3) Delve into the importance of listening attentively
4) Learn ways to establish rapport
5) Explore the relationship between rapport and influence

Assessing Progress

Course Technology has developed a Crisp Series **assessment** that covers the fundamental information presented in this book. A 25-item, multiple-choice and true/false questionnaire allows the reader to evaluate his or her comprehension of the subject matter. To buy the assessment and answer key, go to www.courseilt.com and search on the book title or via the assessment format, or call 1-800-442-7477.

Assessments should not be used in any employee-selection process.

About the Author

A seasoned businesswoman, educator, writer, and consultant, Elaina Zuker has held executive positions in publishing, higher education, manufacturing, and communications. She has served on the faculties of Montclair State College (Division of Business), Mercy College, Pace University, and Marymount College. And she serves as director of the membership drive for the National Association for Female Executives.

Her newest book, *The Seven Secrets of Influence* (McGraw-Hill), a "main selection" for the Business Week Book Club, has been translated into seven languages. Elaina is also the author of *Mastering Assertiveness Skills* and *The Assertive Manager* (AMACOM). Her book for Crisp Publishing's Fifty-Minute Book Series, *Influence*, has been used by many corporations and organizations as a training and development resource. She also has created custom publications for *Time, Money, Inc., Working Woman,* and many other magazines.

Organizations and corporations in the United States and internationally call on Elaina to lecture at their conferences and conventions. She has been a keynote speaker for the Organization Development Network, American Society for Training and Development, Direct Selling Association, International Association of Business Communicators, Hotel Sales and Marketing Association International, and Association of Association Executives. She also has been featured on numerous radio and television talk shows and in many newspaper articles.

Elaina holds a B.S. in psychology from Empire State College and an M.S. in organizational behavior/management from New York Polytechnic Institute.

Preface

The idea for this book came from a seminar I created and conducted with groups of managers and professionals in corporations all over America. It's based on real work with real people who need real hands-on skills to help them in their daily interactions, as they attempt to work together in the increasingly tough and competitive environments of most organizations today.

With a team of organizational psychologists, I did some research, interviewing people in different groups and departments. I discovered that most training programs were directed at managers or executives. The training that was offered to professionals and "individual contributors" was usually informational, intended to help them further develop their technical skills.

What they really needed to complete their proficiency in managing and completing projects was a set of missing skills—rapport skills. As a result, I developed a rapport skills program and then a "train the trainer" program, for a wider audience.

The many benefits of learning about rapport skills include:

- Understanding and tuning in to how people process information so you can become a more insightful and powerful communicator
- Learning refined listening skills and finely tuned attentiveness
- Discovering other people's decision-making strategies
- Enhancing your ability to influence other people's decisions
- Developing a more flexible behavioral and communication repertoire

I believe rapport is a set of skills that you can learn, practice, and master. Use this book as a guide, practicing different techniques with different people, and you will find that you will improve your rapport and communication skills.

Good luck and much success in your journey to improve rapport!

Table of Contents

Part 4: Setting the Stage to Influence Others 51

Part 5: The Formula for Success 67

Appendix 81

P A R T 1

The Positive Power of Rapport

2

Creating Rapport

Defining Rapport

What exactly do we mean by rapport? The word *rapport* comes from the French word *rapprochement*, which means "establishing or restoring of harmony and friendly relations."

Rapport is the feeling of trust and comfort we have when we are with someone who knows, hears, understands, accepts, and values us. Some people call it chemistry. It is usually the result of a close association between people who have had shared experiences or who share a common philosophy or background.

Sometimes rapport comes quickly. You may have shared interests or the person may remind you of someone with whom you already have rapport. But usually it takes years to develop.

Rapport is the foundation of most of our relationships. Without it, we feel distant, removed, or out of synch with someone, even if we otherwise have high regard or respect for the person. With rapport, we may disagree or see some things differently from the other person, but we still feel that we have a connection, an identifiable bond. Sometimes rapport develops even between people who have very little in common.

If you have feelings of rapport with many people and get positive feedback from others, you are probably already practicing at least some of the techniques discussed in this book—although you may not be conscious of it.

Misconceptions vs. Reality

Many people think there is something magical about rapport. "It's kind of hard to explain," they say. "Even when we don't discuss something, I always know just how the other person feels."

You may sometimes feel just the opposite: "I have rapport with some people, but with others, I just don't. No matter what I do or say, I can't make a connection with certain people."

There are a lot of mistaken beliefs and misunderstandings about what rapport is and what it is not. Let's examine some common misconceptions—and the realities.

Misconception: *I agree with the subject the other person is talking about, so we have rapport.*

Reality: You may create a mood of rapport and harmony with someone even if the two of you do not agree on the subject at hand.

Misconception: *Rapport is the same as communication.*

Reality: Not everything you say and do is geared toward rapport. Sometimes we are simply getting along with people. Rapport skills are a subset of communication skills—but they are the key foundation in any communication

Misconception: *Real managers don't need rapport.*

Reality: Like real men don't eat quiche? That used to be true, but it is not anymore, as you will see in this book. These days, all managers need to create rapport in their everyday encounters with their peers, subordinates, managers, colleagues, and suppliers to accomplish their goals more effectively. The old style of "command management" simply does not work anymore.

Misconception: *Rapport comes naturally or it does not happen at all.*

Reality: You will see through this book that, by learning and using a series of simple skills and techniques, you can achieve rapport even with a person you do not like or agree with.

Your Own Reality of Rapport

So what does rapport mean to you? Write your definition here:

____

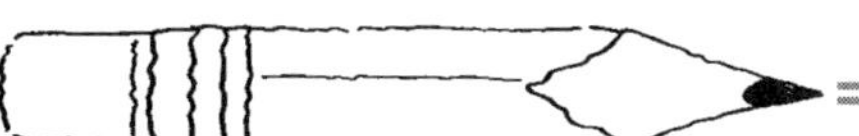

How Do You Feel Rapport?

The point of this exercise is for you to discover what factors or characteristics in a person enable you to develop rapport. You may feel rapport with those who share your values or ideas. You may have mutual friends. You may have similar interests and hobbies. You may discover that what gives you feelings of rapport in one circumstance may not appeal to you in another.

Below is a list of values or tendencies that many people say are the kinds of things that give them feelings of harmony and rapport with others. Place a check (✔) in the yes or no box for each factor to indicate which ones are important to you in establishing rapport.

I have feelings of rapport when:	**Yes**	**No**
I trust the other person.	❑	❑
The person exhibits logic and common sense.	❑	❑
There is an appeal to my intuition.	❑	❑
We have similar values.	❑	❑
We share the same visions for the future.	❑	❑
We have had similar experiences.	❑	❑
We speak the same "language."	❑	❑
We have the same sense of humor.	❑	❑
We like the same people.	❑	❑
We dislike the same people.	❑	❑
We have similar work habits.	❑	❑
We have similar ethics and morals.	❑	❑

CONTINUED

CONTINUED

We speak the same "language."	❑	❑
We have the same sense of humor.	❑	❑
We like the same people.	❑	❑
We dislike the same people.	❑	❑
We have similar work habits.	❑	❑
We have similar ethics and morals.	❑	❑
We agree on philosophy and politics.	❑	❑
We have similar feelings about risk and adventure.	❑	❑

Identifying What It Takes to Establish Rapport

Everyone wants rapport. But how do you get it? Like the weather, rapport is usually noticed only by its outcome. When you have rapport with someone, you just "know" you have it. But the methods or strategies you used to get it are usually instinctive. You often are not sure exactly what you did that worked.

Because we generally are not aware of how we create rapport with other people, it is easy to believe that this ability is a mysterious gift or talent—you either have it or you do not. But anyone can develop rapport. You will see in this book that building rapport involves a set of interpersonal skills that can be learned, practiced, and mastered.

When Do You Have Rapport?

It is easy to see rapport as a process if you think of a personal situation. Think of a time when you were "in harmony" or "in synch" with another person. It may have been with a teacher, a friend, or a stranger you just met. Close your eyes and replay the scene in your mind and try to recall the verbal and nonverbal communication. What did that person say or do that added to your feeling of rapport?

- Did you share the same history and backgrounds?
- Were there words or phrases that seemed similar to your own use of language?
- Did you have the same interests?
- Did you espouse the same ideas and values?
- Did you have similar visions and goals for the future?

A Pattern of Synchronicity

Are you starting to see a pattern? Do you see how many qualities or experiences you had with this person that were the *same* or *similar*? Isn't this the very meaning of being in synch—the very definition of rapport?

The process through which two or more units become synchronized is called *entrainment*. If you apply entrainment to your interactions, you will find that you can establish rapport with almost anyone, even people with whom you never thought you could connect. The next sections explain this concept in more detail.

Building Rapport Through Synchronicity

It is true that real rapport—a true meeting of the minds—usually comes when you have a close relationship with someone. But there are ways to achieve rapport with another person quickly while you are waiting for a deeper dimension to develop. The simple principle of *entrainment* is the basis for rapport.

The Discovery of Entrainment

In 1665, Dutch scientist Christian Huygens noticed that two pendulum clocks, mounted side by side on a wall, would swing together in precise rhythm. They would hold their mutual beat far beyond their capacity to be matched in mechanical accuracy. It was as if they *wanted* to keep the same time—a "mechanical rapport." From Huygens' investigations came the first explanation of what was to be called "mutual phase-locking" of two oscillators, a scientific way of defining entrainment.

The phenomenon, it turns out, is universal. Whenever two or more oscillators in the same field pulse at *nearly* the same time, they tend to lock in so that they pulse at *exactly* the same time. Why? Scientists have concluded that nature seeks the most efficient energy state, and it takes less energy to pulse in cooperation than in opposition. It is most economical to have periodic events that are close in frequency occur in step with one another.

Itzhak Bentov, in his book *Stalking the Wild Pendulum*, described this same phenomenon. He recalled an experiment with two tuned violins. One was placed on a table. A violinist played a note on the other one. The same string that was being played on the one violin was humming on the violin on the table.

Entrainment is found in humans as well. Many examples of matching rhythm are all around us, such as the following:

- A baby's heartbeat synchronizes with that of its mother.
- A powerful public speaker causes the hearts of listeners to beat in rhythm with his.
- Members of an orchestra, all playing different instruments, move, indeed almost breathe, as one.
- Synchronized heartbeats have been reported between psychiatrist and patient.
- Female college roommates sometimes find their menstrual cycles synchronized.
- Physical activities such as singing, rowing, or even marching synchronize the breathing of everyone in the group.

Entrainment and the Rhythm of Rapport

How do concepts of entrainment apply to rapport? Through studies of conversational sequences between people, Dr. William Condon of Boston University School of Medicine concluded that the more you move *in rhythm* with someone, the closer you become with that person. In conversations between two people, he observed the listener moving in precise, shared synchronicity with the speaker—a form of entrainment. This appears to be a universal characteristic of human communications and perhaps of animal behavior in general. Dr. Condon called this the *conversational dance*.

Indeed, communication is like a dance, with everyone engaged in intricate and shared movements across many subtle dimensions, yet all strangely oblivious to what they are doing. Even total strangers display this synchronization. A listener usually does not move as much as a speaker; there are moments when the listener remains quite still. If the listener does move, however, the movements tend to be synchronous with the speaker's activity.

Shifting Rhythms Toward Rapport

Even when pairs or groups start out aggressively toward one another, a shift in rhythms can sometimes occur. Dr. Paul Byers of Columbia University uncovered an example of this with a tribe in South America known as the Fierce People. When the two village chieftains first encounter each other, they yell and scream and gesture wildly. The two men's pitch and energy levels are very similar. Although the confrontation looks and sounds like an angry shouting match, the content of what they are saying gradually becomes less important. In the end, they feel less hostile toward each other.

Although many people decry small talk as frivolous and urge us to get to the point, small talk often functions as a necessary overture to entrainment, a prelude to establishing rapport.

The entrainment described here is like a human law of gravity. Personnel specialist Edgar B. Wycoff noted that with a slight modification, Newton's Law would express a human truth: "One person's thoughts are attracted to another person's thoughts with a force directly proportionate to the similarity of their experiences."

To establish rapport with someone, regardless of whether you agree with the *content* of the person's communication, the most expeditious and effective way is consciously to seek entrainment with that person. This will lead to instant rapport, which provides the ideal setting for your communication.

PART 2

The Growing Need for Rapport in Business Today

Conducting Business Amid Continual Change

Whether you are a rookie in today's workplace or a seasoned veteran, you will be playing by a different set of rules than your parents or grandparents did. And these changing "rules" have led to a greater need for rapport-building skills.

Behind these new rules are six business trends that are changing the way companies operate and which require people to influence without control:

- Ever-increasing competition
- The use of technology and the perils of depersonalization
- The quickening flow of information
- More open communication throughout the organization
- Flatter organization structure
- Cross-departmental teams

This part looks at what these changes mean in the business environment and explores why rapport-building is a key skill in business, now more than ever.

For more information about working through organizational transitions, read *Managing Change at Work*, by Cynthia D. Scott and Dennis T. Jaffe, a Crisp Series book by Thomson Learning.

Responding to Increasing Competition

Companies of all sizes nowadays emphasize streamlining, consolidating, downsizing, containing costs, and belt tightening to make the company more attractive to investors or to guard against takeovers.

What this means for employees is scarcer resources. You face hotter and hotter competition with your colleagues for basic resources that you need to do your job, such as budgets, equipment, and support staff. On a personal level, this trend means increased competition for project approvals, for choice assignments, for management's attention, and for the extras that you once may have taken for granted.

Building Rapport to Stay Competitive at Home and Abroad

Successfully competing within a company as an individual, however, does not mean anything unless the company itself is competitive. And today, rapport building is essential to maintaining competitiveness in national and world markets.

Rapport-building skills are a necessary part of the job, whether you are in marketing, public relations, sales, accounting, or purchasing. Knowing how to work well with people who control resources is to your advantage—and to your company's. Such skills are key to surviving in today's restrictive business atmosphere.

Another dimension to this picture is cultural diversity. Your suppliers, buyers, investors, and partners may be from a different culture. The unified European marketplace and developing countries jockey for position in the global economy. You may be doing business with foreign-owned companies, foreign subsidiaries of your own company, or the overseas headquarters of your own company.

All this means increased global competition. You are competing with and working for people who have different customs, cultural backgrounds, and communication habits. Finely tuned rapport and communication skills offer the only way to ensure success in this environment.

Meeting "High-Touch" Needs in High-Tech Times

Today's global economy is made possible by new communication technology, another area of far-reaching change. These technologies are completely changing how business is conducted. We are now connected as never before.

Wanted: One-on-One Skills for the New Team Environment

The gap between the technically knowledgeable and the technologically naive continues to widen. As a result, people who have technical jobs work more often on multifunction teams or task forces. More jobs require interdepartmental teams, or teams made up of people who do not typically work together and who may not even work at the same job site.

John Naisbitt, author of the best-seller *Megatrends 2000*, points out, however, that our high-tech capabilities have raced ahead of our "high-touch" needs. We are investing increasingly larger blocks of time and energy in learning how to use new technologies most effectively. But as our communication becomes more technical, we are spending less time developing the interpersonal communication skills (the rapport skills) that enable us to produce the best product or provide the best service we can.

With the technological ways we communicate (e-mail, voice mail, video conferencing), we cannot always meet face-to-face to fine-tune our rapport skills. But you cannot get agreement or support for what you want without communicating your desires clearly.

For more information on developing interpersonal skills in the electronic age, read *Face-to-Face Communication*, by Kathleen Begley, a Crisp Series book by Thomson Learning.

Getting the Information You Need

Try to imagine the marketplace 40 years ago. No copy machines, no overnight mail, and no modems to connect you with suppliers or clients. Managers had much less information to work with. Today's increase in technology has prompted a parallel increase in information. Information now comes in mind-boggling quantities and at split-second speeds. And as we rapidly move from an industrial economy based on manufacturing to a service economy, the flow of information only quickens.

Information Flow

Yet the problem is not the overflow of information but the distribution of this information throughout an organization. Getting information to the right person at the right time can mean the success or failure of major deals. And it can save enormous amounts of money that would otherwise be spent duplicating efforts. Getting all the information you need also presents new challenges.

It is like putting together a jigsaw puzzle. There are people who have some pieces of it. But to complete the puzzle—to get the whole picture—you must acquire the rest of the pieces from other people. The secret of success is being able to gain the cooperation of all the right people. And that is where the need for communication, rapport, and influencing without control comes in.

Communicating Openly Throughout the Organization

In the not-too-distant past, individuals worked autonomously. They rarely knew what the next person up the ladder in their own company did—much less what people in other companies did.

Now information on how we do our jobs has become more accessible. We are not as guarded as we once were. There is less physical space and less job differentiation between us and the people below and above us. As a result, employees are developing different job expectations. This represents a radical change in worker values.

Employees no longer tolerate bossy managers who act like dictators or commanding officers. Instead of simply following arbitrary orders, workers want to take part actively in decision making. This new expectation has created a need for a different type of manager.

The most successful managers today are more open and encourage participation and two-way communication. Managers who remain closed or secretive risk alienating people above them and below them in the organizational structure. Companies now look for managers with the right people skills. These skills, of course, include rapport-building skills.

Working Creatively and Implementing New Ideas

The new work force of more responsive and responsible workers and more open managers has increased the demand for internal innovation. More and more companies are demanding increased creativity from their workers in return for increased career control.

Companies are looking for innovative ideas in internal structure as well as for external competition. Workers and managers are asked to become "intrapreneurs"—innovators who work *inside* a corporate structure to create smaller business units that operate almost independently of the parent organization.

No longer is creativity the exclusive province of the marketing or advertising departments. In today's most successful companies, all areas—manufacturing, management information systems, accounting, human resources, and research and development—are hotbeds of innovation and creativity.

Successfully implementing these new ideas and creative solutions calls for highly developed communication skills. Innovators need the ability to sell an idea and to influence without control. We have all seen a great idea die a premature death or gather dust in a file drawer because its creator lacked the communication and rapport skills to persuade the right players and to get people "on board."

Forming Relationships Amid Reorganization

The five areas discussed so far in which business has changed—competition, technology, information, open communication, and innovation—have contributed to a sixth change: reorganization. Corporations are undergoing sweeping structural changes that cut across industry lines, geography, and corporate size. People are now required to persuade and influence others without having official authority or control over them.

The Pyramid Flattens

Companies traditionally were formally structured from the top down in a strict military or hierarchical model. Upper management sat at the top of a pyramid, with varying layers of middle managers in the middle, and a broad base of supervisors and workers below. Orders issued at the top filtered down through the organization. A single group of top individuals made decisions, and the influence was top-down.

Today, however, the way companies work is becoming less formal, and relationships throughout a typical organization are starting to change. Companies are taking decentralization to its logical conclusion, and the corporate structure itself is changing.

The layers of middle management—the corporate overseers—are being reduced in some companies by as much as 80 percent, according to some estimates. In one study of top corporations, those with the best performance records had fewer than four management layers. Those with the worst had as many as eight. Many U.S. organizations now are "outsourcing" entire departments or divisions, sometimes to far-flung corners of the globe such as India or the Philippines.

The result is that workers who used to interact primarily with those within a small radius of their own position are communicating more and more throughout the organization, perhaps even across the country and around the globe.

Traditional Hierarchical Communication Structures

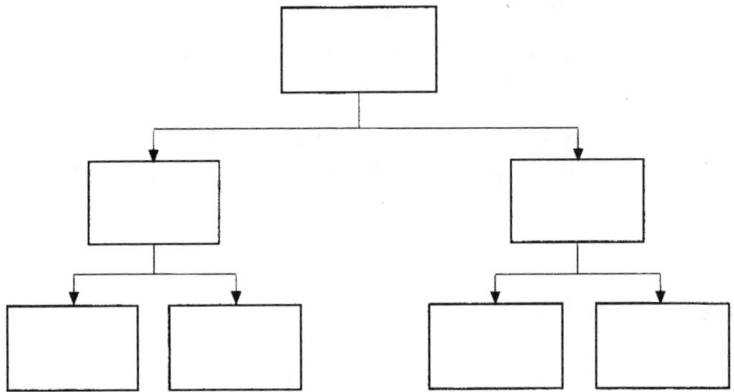

Characterized by:

- Subordinate-boss relationships
- Decisions made at top, executed below
- Management skills: Leadership, planning, controlling, organizing, and integrating people and resources for efficient and effective work production, coaching, counseling, goal and task definition, performance appraisal

Problems solved by:

- Authority
- Procedure
- Management decision

Decisions are:

- Made by single person or with the consensus of a small group of specialists
- Implemented by direction

Relationships are:

- Defined by structure based on loyalty, obedience, leadership

New Rapport Structures

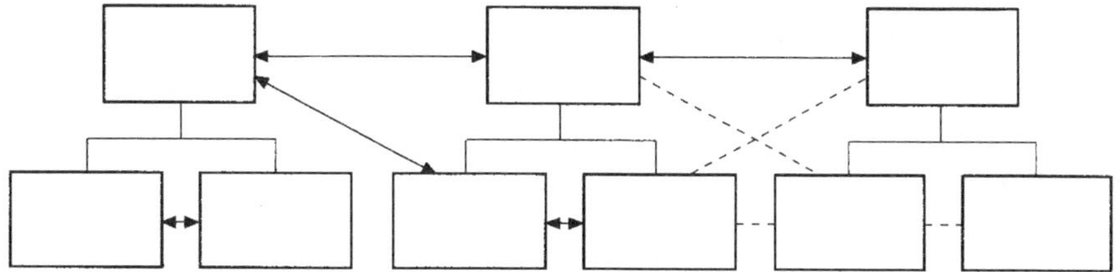

Characterized by:

- Peer, no-authority relationships
- Decisions made by collaboration and involvement
- Management skills: Linking people by being supportive, helpful; sharing power; building trust to serve mutual interests; sharing resources, advice, and aid; performing work efficiently and effectively

Problems solved by:

- Using support and help to establish ground rules for efficiently handling issues

Decisions are:

- Made by sharing power so that alternatives are offered from diverse perspectives and systematically evaluated
- Made by collaboration and using influence without control

Relationships are:

- Based on mutual trust

Changing the Way We Communicate

If you are in the middle of an organization, you are caught between those above you, whom you are supposed to serve, and those below you, whom you must *manage*. In both cases, you must build rapport and exert influence to get the results you want, even though you may not have the organizationally sanctioned power or authority to do so.

So, as a manager or worker, the demands on you are considerable:

- You have to work through others with whom there are often no clear reporting relationships
- You often have more responsibility than authority
- You may have no clearly defined goals or criteria for your success

In today's flatter organizational structures, the way things get done, especially by people in the middle and by staff or "individual contributors," is through rapport building.

Coercion or formal authority, useful in the old model, is no longer effective. Your influence must be subtle and sincere to get decisions made *upward* with managers, *downward* with subordinates, and *laterally* with peers and co-workers.

Shifts in corporate structures mean people have to work with others without benefit of a clear reporting relationship. Thus, you have to gain rapport with people over whom you have no formal authority. The way you communicate must change when decisions require support and participation from others who have the resources, skills, and information you need.

Using Management Authority vs. Rapport Skills

The need for good rapport-building skills is likely to expand amid the major structural changes taking place in business today. But this does not mean you should eliminate old management skills from your repertoire. Certain circumstances clearly require rapport and others require traditional management authority.

There is no question that when decisions require support and participation from others outside your sphere of authority, rapport skills are called for. But in other situations, traditional management authority can be exercised. The situation and circumstances determine the right communication method, as shown in the table on the next page.

Management Skills vs. Rapport Skills

Management Skills Are Required When:	**Rapport Skills Are Required When:**
Decisions are unilateral	Decisions call for participation and support
You are in control of people, resources, projects	Others have expertise, information, contacts, or resources you need to get results
Issues are simple, predictable, linear	Issues are complex, unpredictable, nonlinear
Impact is on single units or departments	Impact is on multiple units ("ripple effect")
Impact and concerns are narrow, contained	
Results are obtained by controlling, directing, evaluating	Organizational impact and concerns are broad
Structures are preset	Results are obtained by spontaneity and responsiveness to organizational needs
You have official recognition	Structures emerge from assessing issues and setting goals
You have extrinsic power	You need informal support, intrinsic power
You work with autonomy	Success is achieved through interdependence
The "territory" is defined and contained	There is territorial overlap
You are directing	You are negotiating, persuading

What's Your Perspective?

As you work through this book and learn about rapport building, think about the people you work with and their relationship to you. Apply the skills directly to these relationships because they are the most immediately important to you.

For this exercise, draw a diagram of *your* organization, using boxes and lines to indicate reporting structures as in the sample diagrams discussed earlier. Be sure to put yourself in the chart.

My Organization

CONTINUED

CONTINUED

Now answer the following questions as they apply to your organization:

1. What are the underlying forces that have created this structure? Think about the trends in the new work environment. Which of these has had the greatest effect on your company, and why? ______________________________

____

2. On the lines below, write the names of three people in the boxes (positions) that are connected to yours by a line in your diagram. Next, ask yourself what the major differences are between you and the people in the adjoining boxes. Do they have more or different skills? More or less power? Write these differences next to each name below. ____________________

____

3. What do you have in common with these people? Do they have the same skills? Are you on the same level? Describe these on the lines below. (These commonalities will be crucial when you begin to make a rapport plan.)

____

4. Is each of these people resistant to you or receptive to you? If any are resistant to you, state why. Are there power differences? A personality clash? Describe differences or conflicts on the lines below. ____________

____

Getting Ahead in the Age of Change

Changes in the business environment are bringing about another set of radical changes. These are the changes in the way we deal with our careers.

It's Not What You Know

It used to be that when we started up the corporate ladder, to achieve success we needed simply to put in our time and to develop professional and technical expertise.

It's Not Who You Know

After a while, this began to change and we heard that "it's not what you know; it's who you know." We began to learn the importance of contacts, and how to build a network of helpful people.

So What Is It?

This is a new era. It is not enough to count on technical or professional expertise alone. These skills can become obsolete quickly. And you cannot count on your contacts to get you what you want. High-level contacts can vanish overnight with the next corporate shake-up, budget cut, acquisition, or merger.

What you need is something of your own, an inner resource or ability that you can tap whenever it is called for. What you need, in short, is *rapport*—a set of people skills that can serve you whenever and wherever you are, a set of interpersonal skills that you can practice anytime, anywhere, inside or outside an organization.

Let's look at setting goals to develop these people skills.

FORMULATING YOUR RAPPORT GOALS

Before beginning any new enterprise, it is always a good idea to establish specific goals. What would you be able to accomplish if you had more rapport with more people? How would things be different? Place a checkmark (✔) by the goals that are important to you.

- ❑ "Read" other people and situations better.
- ❑ Be flexible.
- ❑ Get cooperation from previously adversarial individuals or groups.
- ❑ Persuade others to support projects.
- ❑ Get more information from people when it is needed.
- ❑ Have more credibility with others.
- ❑ See ideas inside as well as outside my immediate department or group.
- ❑ Communicate better within my department and with my manager.
- ❑ Listen and respond better to others.
- ❑ Learn new ideas and apply those ideas in communication.
- ❑ Communicate more effectively with others outside my immediate group.
- ❑ Become more effective at meetings.
- ❑ Keep meetings moving productively.
- ❑ Learn to get more information from people in my organization.
- ❑ Become more aware of and open to the different styles of those I work with.
- ❑ Learn how to create cooperation.
- ❑ Identify and expand my base of supporters.
- ❑ Get my projects supported by upper management.
- ❑ Become aware of more options, so I don't get "stuck."
- ❑ Other goals?____

____

Developing a Rapport Action Plan

A rapport action plan will help you focus more specifically on your rapport-building goals.

You will be able to pinpoint a short-term, specific goal for that one person or situation that currently represents a challenge for you. Later, you may want to return to this plan to change, refine, or update it.

A Five-Step Plan

Step 1 **TARGET the person or people with whom you want to build rapport.** Is it your boss? A peer? A subordinate? Someone who you want to influence, although you have no formal control over him/her? Or is it a person or group that has the power to stop your promotion or eliminate your pet project from the schedule?

Step 2 **IDENTIFY the situation to be changed.**
Is it an action? Maybe it is inaction. Maybe you want this person or group to be more open with you. Or perhaps you would like to clear up a misunderstanding.

Step 3 **ENVISION a positive outcome**.
Is your desired outcome simply to fulfill your immediate goal? Or will there be some long-term effect—either positive or negative?

Step 4 **CREATE benchmarks to measure success.**
What measurable, observable evidence will you need to ensure that you have fulfilled your goal? Will the person be friendlier? Will the group be more open to your suggestions? Measuring results is critical to gauging success. Too many people overlook this important aspect of establishing rapport.

Step 5 **SET deadlines.**
Determine when you can realistically expect to develop rapport with this person or group and fulfill your goal. It can be a year or six months from now—or even next week. But set a real date and stick to it.

This plan reminds you to achieve the goal you have set for yourself. You can also use this format as a model for setting future rapport-building goals.

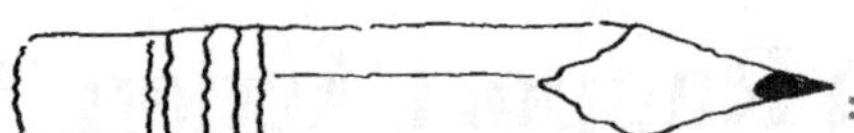

YOUR ACTION PLAN

Think about what you would be able to accomplish if you had more rapport with more people. How would things be different? This exercise is designed to help you get started by pinpointing a specific, short-term rapport goal with one person. Then use this template repeatedly to take action in building rapport with others.

1. *Whom* do I want to establish rapport with?

   ____

2. *What* behavior do I want to change in this person?

   ____

   ____

3. *What* will result if I manage to achieve rapport in this relationship?

   ____

   ____

4. *How* will I know the result has been achieved?

   ____

   ____

5. *When* will I achieve rapport with this person and fulfill this goal?

   ____

   ____

PART 3

The Art of Listening: The Foundation of Rapport

The Challenge of Listening Attentively

Your attitude toward listening is as important as the skill of listening itself. It sounds like such an easy thing to do, but listening is not a passive exercise. It requires having an open mind and a genuine interest in others, as you will learn by working through this part of the book.

Roadblocks to Effective Listening

Many people think that all that is required for listening is keeping your mouth shut and your ears open. But *really* keeping our ears open seems to be a Herculean task for many of us. Why? Common barriers to effective listening include:

- **Distractions**

  A multitude of interruptions and diversions—both internal and external—can keep us from paying close attention.

- **Lack of Training**

  Sometimes we simply tune out. The mind of an untrained listener often randomly voyages across a vast uncharted territory of thought while appearing to pay close attention, even to the point of adding such appropriate responses as "really," "yes," and "uh-huh."

- **Filtering**

  Sometimes our inability to listen—to hear what people are actually telling us—occurs because we generally perceive the world in ways that reflect our own needs.

- **Self-Absorption**

  We are often preoccupied with our own agenda. While the other person is speaking, we are busy planning what we want to say and mentally rehearsing our responses.

Listening to Achieve Rapport

Developing new attitudes and approaches toward listening—and practicing them—are the "power tools" of building rapport. After all, how can you achieve "harmony" with others whom you know nothing about? Finding common ground—synchronicity—begins with listening to what they have to say, expressing interest, asking good questions, and then listening to the answers. Building rapport begins and ends with listening.

This part examines listening and communication techniques as they apply to establishing and building rapport.

Listening with an Open Mind

The Japanese symbol for the word *listen* is composed of the character for "ear" placed within the character for "gate." This pictograph makes sense. When we listen to people, we are, in effect, passing through their gate and entering their world.

Taking a Risk

When we are really listening, we are receiving other people's attitudes in an open, nonjudgmental way. Being so open-minded can be risky because the speaker's point of view may challenge our own. It takes courage, but it is worthwhile because to listen well is to view the world from another person's vantage point.

To listen in a truly open, nonjudgmental way requires a lot of inner security. Most of us are afraid to listen in this way because we believe that we might be *changed*, that our beliefs may be altered, or that we may lose our identity.

But all that is required to listen in this way is *acceptance*, not necessarily *agreement*. Even when you really hear another person out, you can always return to your own beliefs and opinions. But first, you must listen with an open mind.

If people sense through your verbal and nonverbal behavior that you are listening openly and acceptingly, they will feel far less threatened by you and will be much more open. Lines of defense drop. Consequently, people will feel freer to explore other angles or options—and will be much more receptive to what *you* have to say.

By listening to another person openly, you convey a forceful message. You say, "I'm interested in you as a person, and I think what you have to say is important. I'm not trying to judge or evaluate you. I respect your thoughts; and even if I don't agree with them, I know that they are valid for you."

When you practice this kind of listening, you will find attitudes and behavior are contagious. If you listen actively and respectfully, chances are that you will be *listened* to respectfully when it is your turn to speak.

Developing a Genuine Interest in Others

Really listening to others requires an attitude of sincere interest and curiosity and an honest desire to see things the way that others see them. It requires that you temporarily suspend judgment—that, for the moment, you ignore yourself and your attachment to your own ideas.

Imagine, for example, that you are visiting another planet and the individual with whom you are speaking is an intelligent being you have discovered there. Simply gather information. What does the extraterrestrial look like, sound like? What does the being talk about? Remember—do not evaluate what you perceive, and do not judge it, even to yourself, as good, bad, stupid, smart, or silly. Just observe.

Once you have trained yourself to listen in this way, you will see and hear things you would have overlooked before. You may find that people are more intriguing or interesting to you. Ignore your urge to decide whether you like them, whether they are like you, or whether they fit into your frame of reference. If you can suspend judgment, you are apt to discover a better sense of rapport with others.

Listen as if you are doing research on all the different aspects of this person's communication—choice of words, pet phrases, nonverbal cues, hot buttons, and the like. Even the side trips that people take in their communication can be informative and revealing. You can store them in your "data bank" for reference later when you need rapport in particular situations.

Asking Good Questions

Sometimes even when you want to know more about another person, you may hesitate to ask questions because you fear that it seems nosy. Usually, however, the converse is true. Most people feel complimented when they are asked questions. They are flattered that someone is expressing interest in them.

What Are You Curious About?

Asking good questions begins with tuning in to your own curiosity. What do *you* want to know about this person? Once you know *what* you want to ask, use the following tips to get clear, informative answers:

- **Ask open-ended questions**—A shy or reticent person may take the easy way out if your inquiries can be answered with a simple yes or no. For example, rather than "Did you regret making that decision?" ask "How did you feel about making that decision?"
- **Create cycles of learning**—Use some facet of the person's answer to your previous question as a springboard to your next query: "Tell me more about why you decided to launch your own company."
- **Ask for more detail**—Most people speak in generalities. The way to get more interesting, "meaty" information from them is to ask for more detail: "What specifically do you wish you could have done differently?"
- **Avoid turnoff questions**—"How" or "what" questions are usually better received than "why" questions. People often feel defensive when asked to explain their motivations ("why" questions). Often they have not thought through their reasons or they do not want to disclose them.

When you ask people *how* they did something, they are flattered by your interest in the process by which they accomplished something. Sometimes you will also get an interesting inside look at their way of doing things, which can help you in building rapport with them.

Starter Questions

Here are a few general questions that can help get people talking:

- *"What's your understanding of this situation?"*
- *"What are your goals for this project? What outcome are you looking for?"*
- *"I'm wondering ..." I'm curious about ..."*
- *"How did you arrive at that decision?"* or *"What were the most important criteria for you in making that decision?"* (These questions offer you a glimpse of people's decision-making strategies, which can be useful for evaluating their capabilities in a particular area.)
- *"What caused you to ..."* or *"What motivated you to ..."* (Here, you are looking to underlying reasons, motivations, and catalysts to people's decision making.)

Listening Without Advising

Many people believe that just listening without injecting comments or advice seems too passive or compliant. It is curious and unfortunate that people tend to think that any action is better than no action, and that just listening or absorbing means you are a wimp, a procrastinator, or a do-nothing.

Helping Others by Simply Listening

Jack Gibb, an early figure of humanistic psychology, says, "Help isn't always helpful." What this means is that, even with the best intentions, we are often too directive. We tell others what they should or should not do or what worked for us. Although we feel helpful, we may not be helping others to arrive at the best solution for them. Neither do we empower them to come up with their own solutions. Advice and information are usually seen rightly as attempts to change a person. They serve as barriers to self-expression. Ultimately, the advice is seldom taken and the information is discarded.

Suppose someone in your life—your boss, a colleague, your spouse, or a friend—is telling you about a difficult situation she is in. Your simple task is just to listen, *without* doing all the other, non-listening things we tend to do. For example, try not to jump in and tell her about a similar situation you encountered once and how you solved your problem. And try not to refer her to sources where she can find advice or help—until you have first just *listened* to what she has to say.

Or, as another example, a co-worker is very upset about being passed over for a promotion. He has been working for the company for many years, and feels that younger, more technically skilled people are getting more advantages. Your instinct might be to give him advice or suggestions about how he might approach his boss, but the best way you can help him at this time is to just listen. He may very likely come up with ideas or solutions on his own, if you give him some attention and time.

All your recommendations might be useful and well-meaning in their place, but they detract from your simply "being there" for the other person. When people are having troubles or difficulty, often all they really want is someone simply to listen. Chances are, your troubled friend, colleague, or relative knows the solution or can figure it out. What she needs is someone just to be there, like a mirror.

Listening to Promote Understanding

Like any communication technique, listening takes practice. And it takes concentration. There are several forms of listening, and the simplest is *open listening*—being "all ears." One way to check whether you are really hearing what you are being told is to observe, as you are listening, where your mind is going and what you are thinking about.

Try to eliminate the "noise" going on simultaneously in your mind by concentrating more on the other person, and then see what happens to the quality of your conversation.

The following listening techniques are more proactive than open listening. They have the dual advantage of helping you to focus on what the other person is saying and encouraging more precise communication.

Active Listening

An active listener "restates" the content of what is being said. This means putting into your own words the meaning of what was just said. You must be careful, though, not to use the other person's words to express *your* thoughts so that you change the essential meaning. Simply clarify the phrase or sentence, without changing the integrity of what was said.

Try to echo, in words, what the person said. Suppose your friend says to you, "My boss is really giving me a hard time today." You could restate this by responding, "Sounds like your boss is on your case for some reason." You can echo simply to check whether you "got" the communication the way the other person sent it.

Reflecting Feelings

The reflective feelings technique is similar to restating in that you attempt to mirror back what you heard. Instead of restating the ideas, however, you try to reflect the feelings or emotion behind them. For example, if someone says to you, "My friends always ask me to do favors for them as if I have all the time in the world on my hands." To reflect the feelings of this statement, you might say, "You sound angry about that." Here, you are listening for the tone expressed by the spoken words.

Caution: When reflecting feelings, you are only *guessing* at the feelings the person may be having. So you may want to try a few different feeling statements. Then the other person has the chance to let you know whether your sense of his emotion is correct.

Open-Ended Questioning

Open-ended questions are those that do not lend themselves to simple yes or no answers. Usually they begin with *what, why*, or *how*. For example: "What do you think you can do about the person?" "How can your friends learn to be more sensitive to you?" Open-ended questions are a great way to get a person to open up to you.

Applying Listening Techniques

This exercise tests your use of listening techniques. Use a specific situation involving a person with whom you are trying to build rapport.

Choose a partner for this exercise and decide, between yourselves, who will be "A" and who will be "B." "A" goes first, as the "listener" and "B" is the speaker for a pre-decided amount of time (e.g. one minute). Then switch, so that "B" is the listener, and "A" is the speaker. Remember this is an exercise in listening, so the topic the speaker selects isn't really important. Practice only one of these listening techniques at a time until you develop your skills.

1. Open Listening

Listen to exactly what the person is saying. Do not add, edit, or interpret their statements. On the lines below, write down exactly what you heard, one sentence at a time. Then show it to the person you listened to and ask for feedback on how accurately you captured what he or she said.

____

____

____

Now write down all the "noise" you heard in your mind, besides what you listened to from the other person. Once you start noticing this, you can train yourself to edit or screen this out.

____

____

2. Active Listening

On the lines below, restate what the person said. Put it into your own words, being careful not to interpret, analyze, add to, or subtract from what was said. Just clarify.

____

____

____

____

CONTINUED

CONTINUED

3. Reflecting Feelings

Write your "guess" of what the person might have been feeling.

____

____

____

4. Open-Ended Questions

These help you to gather more information than the person gave in his or her first communication. Write your question and then the answer you got.

What? Q: ______________________________

A: ______________________________

How? Q: ______________________________

A: ______________________________

When? Q: ______________________________

A: ______________________________

Why? Q: ______________________________

A: ______________________________

Who? Q: ______________________________

A: ______________________________

Clarifying Communication with Blockbusting Questions

People often speak in generalities and they believe you know clearly what they mean. Asking *blockbusting* questions "breaks through" to the true meaning and gets you more precise, more specific information. Blockbusting questions help you eliminate ambiguities.

Here is a simple illustration: Take the statement, "Let's work out an agenda." If someone said this to you in a work context, what would it mean? You might understand this as a project and go back to your workspace, *thinking* you knew what the other person meant but not being sure. Then you would scratch your head and try to work out an agenda according to what you thought the person meant.

But unless you checked it out, you could be way off base. What does *agenda* mean to that person? Does it mean the list of events; the speakers; a detailed, step-by-step plan for the meeting; or just an overall outline? What is meant by "work out," and who is going to be responsible for it?

There are various ways to frame questions to get the other person to be more specific. You could ask any of the following questions:

- *"What, specifically, do you mean by ..."*
- *"Can you give me more information?"*
- *"I wonder if you could give me an example of an agenda that worked well at your last meeting?"*
- *"What information would you like included in the agenda?"*

Break Through the Generalities

For each of the statements below, ask yourself blockbusting questions until you get more specific meaning and understanding of the sentence. Write (a) the blockbusting questions and (b) the expanded, fuller statements that your questions elicit.

1. "Let's work out the agenda."

a. Blockbusting question: ______________________________

b. Revised statement: ______________________________

a. Blockbusting question: ______________________________

b. Revised statement: ______________________________

a. Blockbusting question: ______________________________

b. Revised statement: ______________________________

2. "I want to get that out today."

a. Blockbusting question: ______________________________

b. Revised statement: ______________________________

a. Blockbusting question: ______________________________

b. Revised statement: ______________________________

3. "Training should cover most of the policy procedures."

a. Blockbusting question: ______________________________

b. Revised statement: ______________________________

a. Blockbusting question: ______________________________

b. Revised statement: ______________________________

a. Blockbusting question: ______________________________

b. Revised statement: ______________________________

CONTINUED

CONTINUED

4. "Higher visibility will get us the notice we want."

a. Blockbusting question: ______________________________

b. Revised statement: ______________________________

a. Blockbusting question: ______________________________

b. Revised statement: ______________________________

a. Blockbusting question: ______________________________

b. Revised statement: ______________________________

5. "We need to plan for anticipated growth."

a. Blockbusting question: ______________________________

b. Revised statement: ______________________________

a. Blockbusting question: ______________________________

b. Revised statement: ______________________________

a. Blockbusting question: ______________________________

b. Revised statement: ______________________________

Compare your responses to the author's examples in the Appendix.

Qualifying Comparators for More Precision

Comparators are words and phrases used to compare one idea with another. Comparators are often imprecise and unclear. For example, your manager may tell you to be "more productive." But what specifically does that mean? More productive than what? Than I was last year? Last month? More productive than my co-workers?

These are *qualifying* questions that need to be asked to get a clearer understanding of what your manager means. But there are subtler ways to get this information than from such knee-jerk responses.

Qualifying questions must be asked to avoid possible misinterpretation, but there is a way to word these questions to avoid sounding challenging or threatening to the other person. Be direct but ask in a way that indicates you are seeking a better, clearer understanding.

Consider the following examples:

Comparator: *I need you to be more productive.*

Qualifying question: How do you measure productivity?

Comparator: *That's a better way to do it.*

Qualifying question: On what basis do you consider it better?

Comparator: *We've had very good profits this year.*

Qualifying question: When you say "good," what are you comparing it to?

The exercise on the following page will give you the opportunity to try your hand at asking qualifying questions to clarify comparator statements.

Clarifying Comparators

For each of the comparators listed below, write the qualifying question (a) that instinctively comes to mind when you "hear" the comparator. Then rewrite the question in a more diplomatic way that indicates you are seeking a clearer understanding (b).

1. *That's a better way to do it.*

a. Qualifier: ______________________________

b. Qualifier: ______________________________

2. *We've had very good profits this year.*

a. Qualifier: ______________________________

b. Qualifier: ______________________________

3. *I have a better idea.*

a. Qualifier: ______________________________

b. Qualifier: ______________________________

4. *Doing it this way requires less effort.*

a. Qualifier: ______________________________

b. Qualifier: ______________________________

5. *We should set higher standards.*

a. Qualifier: ______________________________

b. Qualifier: ______________________________

Compare your responses to the author's examples in the Appendix.

Cutting Universals Down to Size

Another category of imprecise statements is *universals*, statements that declare that something is absolutely true or false. The way you can "read" a universal in someone's utterances is from the words *always, never, all*, or *none*. These indicate a black-or-white mode of thinking that often leads to hasty generalizations.

To seek precision, you can ask qualifying questions, such as "How do you know all [fill in the blank] are lazy?" or simply "All?" Such questions challenge the notion that what is claimed is always and forever true.

You might also ask, "Can you think of a time when this was not the case?" thereby challenging others to question their own absolute thinking.

Taking the time to ask simple clarifying questions will equip you to be a more powerful listener and better rapport builder.

From Universal to Specific

For each of the statements below, write a qualifying question (a) that might get the person to state the point more specifically. Then, write a revised statement (b) that you would like to elicit as a result of your question.

1. Each supervisor is responsible for her entire department.

a. Qualifier: ______________________________

b. More accurate revision: ______________________________

2. All management is concerned with its profits.

a. Qualifier: ______________________________

b. More accurate revision: ______________________________

3. Everyone here supports one another.

a. Qualifier: ______________________________

b. More accurate revision: ______________________________

4. My supervisor never notices the extra work I do.

a. Qualifier: ______________________________

b. More accurate revision: ______________________________

5. Nobody shows me any respect.

a. Qualifier: ______________________________

b. More accurate revision: ______________________________

CONTINUED

CONTINUED

6. Everyone does the easiest thing.

a. Qualifier: ______________________________

____

b. More accurate revision: ______________________________

____

7. No one can do my job but me.

a. Qualifier: ______________________________

____

b. More accurate revision: ______________________________

____

8. My manager doesn't trust anyone.

a. Qualifier: ______________________________

____

b. More accurate revision: ______________________________

____

9. I can tell you every response she'll make.

a. Qualifier: ______________________________

____

b. More accurate revision: ______________________________

____

10. We can never get what we need from the support staff.

a. Qualifier: ______________________________

____

b. More accurate revision: ______________________________

____

Compare your responses to the author's examples in the Appendix.

PART 4

Setting the Stage to Influence Others

Refining Your Listening to Perceive Others' Needs

Successful salespeople know that no matter how great the product, most people will buy only from people they feel comfortable with. So making a sale begins with establishing rapport with the customer. Without rapport, your influence over most customers is weak or nonexistent.

Successful salespeople also know that no matter how great the product, it is not going to sell unless the buyer has a genuine or perceived need for it. Of course, the good salesperson does not wait for the buyer to recognize his own need. The skilled seller is alert to the subtle cues that signal a customer's true needs and then uses the cues to demonstrate how a particular item or service addresses those needs. How does the seller discover the buyer's needs? Through refined listening.

These are important lessons for all of us, whether we are employed in sales or not. As Kathleen Begley points out in her book, *Writing That Sells*[3], "Information technology, administration, finance, manufacturing, and distribution are all engaged in selling. But rather than tangible products and services, these departments are pushing intangible concepts." The difference is, we usually do not call this selling. But we are, of course, aiming to *influence* others to our point of view.

---

[3] For more information about influencing others to your ideas, read *Writing That Sells*, by Kathleen Begley, a Crisp Series book by Thomson Learning.

Fine-Tuning Your Listening Skills

There are really only two times when most of us listen extremely well:

- **When something truly interests us.** Even then, our ability to listen can be negatively affected, as when we are preoccupied with a problem.
- **When we know we must.** In these situations we generally need specific information—answers to questions such as "How do I get to the highway from here?" or "Doctor, what do the test results mean?"

To be skilled at influencing others, it is important to master the ability to listen effectively in a broad range of circumstances, not just the two situations listed above. Then you will be able to tune in to others when it is important to you—and when it is important to them. This is done through *refined listening*—listening on a more subtle level and focusing on the more elusive elements of communication.

Refined listening consists of three parts:

- **Content:** The substance of the message
- **Context:** The physical setting and circumstances of the communication
- **Medium:** The packaging of the message

The sections that follow examine each of these parts in detail.

Hearing the Content

Content is the substance of the message—what the person is talking about. It is made up of all the words, facts, and ideas in a communication.

With a few straight-shooting people, the content of the message is all there is—they say exactly what they mean. You probably know one or two of these brutally honest people. Some even preface their remarks with "I'm going to level with you...," and what you get from them is a direct opinion on the matter you are discussing.

Too often, however, we act as if content is all there is in our interactions with people. This can sometimes be deceptive because content alone usually does not convey the speaker's entire message.

Depending on the *context*, a story's *content* will take on different meanings. If you talk about a new business idea, a colleague may use this story to encourage you to move ahead. If you discern from the context that she has been feeling dissatisfied with her job, her content (encouraging you to move ahead) may be her way of hinting to you about her own hopes for the future.

The next section explains how to evaluate a communication's context.

Putting the Content into Context

The context of a communication includes both the physical setting where the communication takes place—the *external environment* of the interaction—and the circumstances of the communication with another person, or the *internal environment.*

The External Environment

Work-related communication may take place in your office, someone else's office, or a neutral work environment such as a conference room, or a social setting such as a restaurant. When a conversation takes place on one person's turf, that person has an advantage in negotiation because she feels more comfortable in that environment. If you are on neutral territory, however, then you will interact on a more equal basis, all other things being equal.

The Internal Environment

In any conversation, it is important to evaluate the internal context of the situation. You might ask any of these questions to determine the circumstances of your communication:

- What emotional or intellectual factors are affecting each of you?
- What is going on in your lives at that time?
- What is the emotional setting?
- Is the other person tense or relaxed, feeling secure or shaky, depressed or elated about a recent occurrence, such as a job change?
- What is your relationship with the person?
- Is the person above or below you in the organizational hierarchy?
- Is this a one-time encounter or an ongoing relationship?
- Is the person responding with her own authority or ideas, or is she being influenced by others or by company rules or policies?

The circumstances of your communication can be grouped into six variables—the six Rs: relationship, range, record, reasons, rules, and resistance. Let's look at each of these variables in the next section.

Evaluating the Six Rs of Internal Context

It is easier to evaluate the internal environment with people whom you know well, but it can also be done with people you have just met. The six Rs, as explained below, will guide you in doing so.

- **Relationship**—What is the nature of your relationship? Have you worked together before or are you strangers? Is it strictly business or do you also have a personal friendship? To gauge a relationship, measure two components—longevity and intensity.

  For longevity, consider not only how long you have already worked with (or interacted with) this person, but also how long you expect to work with the person in the future.

  To measure intensity, consider the depth of your relationship. Is it a superficial, nodding acquaintanceship? Or is it a close relationship in which you will be working together as a team or as part of a task force over a given period of time?

- **Range**—What is the range of the other person's authority or responsibility in your discussion and in the organization as a whole? What is the range of his or her network of contacts within and outside of the organization?

- **Record**—What is the other person's history of response to you? What does this person's record for accepting new ideas or proposals reveal? Begin with whatever background information you can gather, and then make your own evidence-based judgment.

- **Reasons**—Be aware of each party's reasons for communicating. To understand a person's motivations, you may have to do a bit of guesswork, especially if you do not know the person well. And you may have to begin with some probing and questioning to uncover the person's real reasons and motivations.

- **Rules**—Limits or boundaries are often expressed in statements that contain words such as *should, shouldn't, must, mustn't, have to, can't, always*, and *never*. Be aware of others' rules, whether they are valid or exist only in another person's head. Valid reasons may be related to company policy, precedent, professional norms, or ethics. Rules that are valid only to one person are constraints that the person believes to exist.

  It is not your job to judge these rules or the person who follows them. Your only task is to listen and to be aware that personal rules represent restrictions and boundaries for that person's behavior.

- **Resistance**—Common in all communication, resistance could be in the form of a foot-dragging response or an out-and-out no. A resistance statement, such as "I'm not sure yet," "We've never done this before," or "We don't have enough time (or money)," usually means that the person is asking for something from you. It could be more information about your proposal, reassurance that he is not making a mistake, or more rewards or benefits to be gained from saying yes to you.

  Effective communicators realize that resistance is a natural part of the influence process. In fact, they welcome it as an important and necessary step. When people encounter resistance their response frequently is to push harder with the same approach. If this was not working in the first place, however, doing more of it will not get you the result you want.

  A more effective way to deal with resistance is to get into agreement or alignment with it, rather than fight it. This *sounds* paradoxical, but in fact, it is an important lesson from the Eastern approach to life—a philosophy based on cooperation and harmony. Aikido, a Japanese martial art, combines techniques from many other Eastern martial arts. The central principle is to *align* yourself with your attacker and to *use* his energy to foil the attack. You move *with*, rather than *against* your opponent, thereby using his energy to strengthen yours. This then puts you into the advantageous position of creating a win-win situation.

  In negotiating, this can often increase your power. If you are seen as a collaborator or a cooperator, people are more likely to continue to deal with you, instead of cutting you off as an unreasonable adversary.

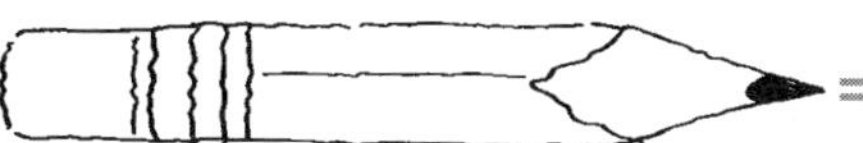

What Is the Internal Context?

For the exercise below, think of a situation in which you want to influence someone. What follows are questions to ask yourself to clarify all dimensions of your relationship—the six Rs—and to give you the basis for future communication.

1. Relationship

How long have you known the person? ____________________

Have you worked together before? ____________________

On a team? ____________________

As a supervisor/subordinate? ____________________

As a colleague? ____________________

Is the relationship strictly business? ____________________

Do you have a personal friendship? ____________________

Do you have things, people, projects in common? ____________________

2. Range

Range of your authority? ____________________

Range of other person's authority? ____________________

Range of other person's network inside and outside the organization?

____

3. Record

His/her response to you in the past? ____________________

How has the person accepted new ideas before? ____________________

4. Reasons

Theirs: ____________________

Yours: ____________________

CONTINUED

CONTINUED

5. Rules

Rules, real and imaginary, that you have heard from the person:

____

Should? ______________________________________

Should not? ___________________________________

Have to? _____________________________________

Can't ____

Always? ______________________________________

Never? _______________________________________

6. Resistance

Statements of resistance you have *already* heard in this situation or are anticipating will come up: ____________________________

____

____

____

Monitoring the Medium

The medium—the packaging of communication—provides the richest area for refined listeners. It is in this "package" that you often get the most valuable information. The external package of a message often has more impact than the message itself. In other words, *how* you are told something is as important as what you are told.

Interpreting Body Language

Bookstores are filled with books on body language. Most of them indicate that a clenched jaw signifies anger, crossing the arms conveys disinterest or boredom, and blushing means embarrassment. The danger in interpreting these signals is generalizing too much. A clenched jaw may not always mean anger. It may indicate stress or a jaw condition. Blushing may not indicate embarrassment. It may signal frustration or anger or nervousness.

Most of us are not trained to notice small bits of behavior unless they produce large changes, and we often misinterpret the changes we do see—such as a clenched jaw or crossed arms. We ascribe meaning to what we see based on our own use of these gestures or the experiences we have had.

You can begin training yourself to notice physiological changes. But do not generalize. Keep your observations specific to each person you are interacting with. If there are five people at a meeting, you may see five different sets of encoded, nonverbal behavior. What may seem like the same nonverbal response in two people may signal something very different about each person's internal state. Just notice and observe. Do not try to interpret or attribute any meaning to what you see.

Tuning In to What's Unspoken

Body language can even be more indicative of a person's true state than the spoken word. There are several categories of nonverbal, unconscious, physiological responses that people exhibit and that you can look for. Usually these are actions outside of a person's conscious awareness. The most important and easily visible ones are the following:

Posture and Gestures

By paying attention to posture and gestures, you can discover when a person is feeling supportive, interested, bored, disagreeable, or in some other mood. These body signals include:

- Sudden straightness of the spine
- Position of the head
- Position of the feet on the floor
- Distribution of weight on hips and lower legs
- Hand movements and gestures

As an experiment, the next time you are having a conversation with someone you know well, note as many of these signals as you can. At different times you may see the person's weight shift, moving from one leg to the other. For this individual, this posturing may indicate a change of mood or internal state—though for another person, it may indicate something else.

Make a friend or colleague your research population of one. Watch nonverbal signals closely. After you practice, it will be difficult for your subject to fool you, despite the words being spoken. You will have gathered indisputable evidence of what the person's body does outside of his conscious control or awareness.

It is critical that your observations be descriptive, not evaluative. Your initial mental or written note should be "left leg weight shift," not "Kyle seems nervous!" In time, you will begin to associate a particular posture or gesture with its corresponding internal state. You will pick up on more subtle but also easily detectable changes once you begin noticing them.

Skin-Color Changes

If you watch carefully, you can begin to see different colorations in a person's face at different times. For example, note the contrast between nose color and the skin color of the forehead. Blushes, of course, are easy to spot, but a blush is not always in the cheeks. Watch for these different areas of blushing:

- At the tip of the ears
- On the forehead
- At the jawline

The blush may be rosy and soft, a purplish pink all over the face, or blotchy red. Some people blush when they are embarrassed, some when they are angry, others when presented with a challenge, and still others when they are sexually excited. Again, your purpose as a refined listener is not to assign judgment, but just to observe these changes in any given person.

Muscle Changes

Minute muscle changes are idiosyncratic. Like other physiological responses, they vary widely from person to person. Watch for:

- Muscle tightness or slackness near the edges of the mouth
- Tightness or squinting around the eyes
- Tightness at the jawline
- The formation of creases on the forehead or directly between the eyes
- Lower lip changes

Lower lip changes are the most common of the small muscle changes. Sometimes when people are feeling pressured or uncomfortable, their lower lip tenses. This is where the expression *tight-lipped* comes from. Some people seem to be this way all the time, but on closer observation, you will see that their lips are tighter at some times than at others.

Tightening is not the only kind of lip change. Others changes to look for include fullness, wetness, movement, dryness, size, trembling, shape, texture (smooth or rough), and color.

Breathing Changes

Changes in breathing are an early barometer of someone's mood. The easiest way to observe a person's breathing rate is to watch the up-and-down movement of their chest or abdomen. Sometimes you can even pick up signals by watching the shadow of a person's shoulder against a background wall. You can see the pattern of rising and falling with every breath.

Rapid breathing will mean something about others' internal state only if you have watched them often enough or long enough to know how they breathe when they are excited and when they are calm.

Voice Patterns

Voices have a number of characteristics, any one of which can vary.

- **Tone:** High or low, loud or soft
- **Tempo:** Fast or slow, with certain pauses or without them
- **Volume:** smooth or variable, booming or cooing. Some voices squeak, other voices sing

Again, try not to evaluate what you hear. Notice the range of possibilities and variations in voice among different people and within the same person at different times.

Because there is no visual distraction, telephone conversations offer an excellent opportunity to practice developing your sensitivity to voice changes. To begin, notice just *one* of the dimensions of voice quality: tone, volume, or speed. With practice, you can acquire sensitivity to all of them.

Do not make assumptions about what changes in voice mean. Simply note the changes. When you have gathered enough examples of how individuals' voices alter when they are angry, or how they change when they are confused, then you can test your assumptions by asking them, "How are you feeling about this idea?"

If you can develop this sensory acuity, you can use your finely tuned radar to notice things that most other people do not. You can be a living lie detector and a powerful influencer.

PRACTICE REFINED LISTENING

Think of a person you would like to influence. Practice listening to this person—the topic is not important; focus on the *process* of the communication.

As you are listening, make notes on the body language—movements, postures, and gestures—the other person is expressing. Remember to be descriptive, not evaluative.

Nonverbal Response Inventory

Position of head: ______________________

Position of feet: ______________________

Distribution of weight on hips and lower legs: ______________________

Hand movements and gestures: ______________________

Skin color changes: ______________________

Small muscle changes:

Edges of mouth: ______________________

Corners of the eyes: ______________________

Jawlines: ______________________

Forehead: ______________________

Lower lip: ______________________

Breathing changes:

Slow/quick: ______________________

Rhythmic/uneven: ______________________

Voice patterns:

Tone: ______________________

Tempo: ______________________

Volume: ______________________

PART 5

The Formula for Success

Like Likes Like

The best way to influence people is first to understand how they communicate, which means being attentive to all the various components of individuals' communication. Then your ability to adapt your style to match their communication will help them feel more comfortable.

People are more open and less defensive if you speak their "language." This refers to the key words they use. These are the verbal clues you must learn to recognize.

Think of the factors, characteristics, values, or tendencies you see in others that help you feel rapport with them. What words come to mind?

____

____

____

What style is represented by these words?

____

Suppose, for example, that the key word you listed is *trust*. In other words, the key ingredient that causes you to feel rapport is that you trust the person. Or you may have listed such words as *shared vision* or *brighter future* as the key elements in rapport for you. Some people say yes to another's influence when a clear *benefit* is stated—a benefit that seems to zero in on some need or goal that they, the recipient, have.

People like to be communicated with—and influenced—in a way that feels familiar and comfortable to them.

"Like likes like" is a basic principle in all of nature. The next section explains how you can apply this principle across the communication spectrum to build rapport quickly.

"Pacing" to Accelerate Rapport Building

The most expeditious and effective way to establish and build rapport with someone is consciously to seek entrainment with, or synchronicity with, the person. Another way of saying this is "pacing." That is, even when you are not *naturally* in rapport with someone, by following certain steps and actions, you can *accelerate* the achievement of rapport.

Pacing may be thought of as helping people see or hear themselves. When you get into agreement or alignment with someone, they (often unconsciously) get a feeling of "I trust you" or "you are like me."

Not only does this have a powerful effect on the other person, it also will have a dramatic effect on you. By getting into agreement or alignment with another, you are getting "into" their way of being in the world. In a very real way, you have an experience similar to theirs. If you do this often and well, you will have a deep understanding and empathy with the other person.

You also may find that the word "bored" will leave your vocabulary. Your attention will be so focused on all the elements or "clues" the other person is sending your way that you will become fascinated with how complex and diverse people are.

Begin with Refined Listening

After you have observed the communication elements of refined listening—content, context, and medium—then match, pace, or mirror one or more of the unconscious rhythms or gestures of the other person. Alter your habits to match; pace what you see the other person doing; and mirror the voice, tone, and tempo the other person uses. This will enable you to use all the components of a person's communication to get the best results.

Matching and pacing your rhythms with those of another person are at the heart of influence. Once you are in tune with people, they are far more likely to respond to you and your efforts to influence them. Let's take a look at these techniques.

Matching Breathing

Observation is the first step in matching breathing. Begin by noticing the pattern, pace, and rhythm of the other person's breathing. People breathe high in the chest, or low, or deep in the abdomen. While they are speaking, they breathe fast or slow, with or without pauses. You can gauge people's breathing by observing the rise or fall of their shoulders or the pulse points in their neck or chest.

Then check your own breathing and see which elements (speed, rhythm) are the same or different. Try to synchronize, or *match*, one element at a time. You may notice, for example, that the person is breathing quite slowly. If your breathing pattern is quick, slow it down until it matches the speed of the other person's. Soon you will be able to match more than one element, and you will be breathing in synch with the other person. The person will feel it too.

Matching Voice

In business, the easiest and most successful matching technique involves voice. You can match others' speed or volume or intonation. You must do this with some subtlety, however, or you run the risk that people will think you are mimicking them. And you should not match others' voices with such precision that you sound foreign or radically different from your own speech pattern.

Mirroring Movements and Gestures

Imagine you are meeting an influential client in her office. You want to attain an initial rapport before trying to influence this person. You sit in a chair and place a folder across your lap. She sits rather stiffly and upright in her desk chair. Her hands move constantly, straightening out papers on her desk. Of course, you cannot pace her hand movements because you do not have papers to shift. But you can sit just as stiffly without being in exactly the same position. And you do not want to react immediately; if you do, it will look as if you are mimicking her. As your conversation progresses, work to pace her actions and vocal tones.

In this situation, here is how the pacing and matching would work.

1. She leans across the desk toward you.
   You lean slightly toward her.
2. She leans back in her chair.
   You lean back to your original position.
3. Soon her hands stop moving around. She folds them in front of herself.

You, of course, had your hands that way, on top of a folder in your lap. She is now mirroring you! You now have built a good foundation of rapport by "speaking" the same body language.

Do not expect cues to be immediate. Entrainment happens over a long conversation, so be observant and patient. Remember, too, that you want to approximate these behaviors, not mimic them. You must do it in a subtle way so that it is not noticed. Otherwise, the people you ultimately want to build rapport with will (correctly) think that you are mimicking them.

Mirroring with Words

Often, what is most important is not so much the content of what you present, but the language you use to convey it—not *what* you communicate, but how you communicate it. Mirroring with words is an important way to establish the instant rapport you need to maximize your influence.

Listening for "Representational System"

People perceive the world, process information, and communicate through different sensory channels—through the sense of sight, sound, touch, smell, or taste. Some people, for example, experience life as a series of moving or still pictures. Others focus on sounds, such as voices, music, and noise, as a way to "see" the world. They may remember the words they have heard or their own internal voices. Still others experience life primarily through touching and other body sensations.

Each of us has a preferred sensory channel, or *representational system*. If you listen, you will hear people "telling" you which one they prefer. They will use certain language and figures of speech which, in effect, tell you something about how their minds work.

- *Visual* uses phrases such as "That's the way I see it," "It seems clear to me," or "Let's watch this carefully."
- *Auditory* says "I hear what you're saying," "That rings a bell," or "It doesn't sound right to me."
- *Kinesthetic* uses physical or tactile images. His or her language will include expressions like "I'm getting a grasp on the situation," "When the new policy takes hold …" or "It feels right to me."
- *Gustatory* uses phrases such as "It leaves a good taste in my mouth," "I need to chew on it for a while," or "That's a spicy idea."
- *Olfactory* says "It didn't smell right to me," "This deal smells fishy," or "She came out of it smelling like a rose."

Speaking the Language of Representation System

When you have observed and listened to another person and discovered that his primary mode of experiencing is, say, visual, then the best way to gain rapport is to speak the same language. Match, as well as you can, your mode of expression to that person's mode. Put your questions in language that appeals to the visual: "Can you *see* yourself owning this?" or "Shall I *show* you how it works?" You can also show visuals—graphs, charts, drawings—to a visual person. Simply telling something to a visual person may not be enough.

Similarly, if someone uses an auditory mode of expression, package your communication with auditory-based language: "How does this *sound* to you?" "Do you think this idea has the right *tone*?" or "Will this *ring a bell* with management?"

If it is not readily apparent which form of communication a person prefers, you may have to use the trial-and-error approach. If you do not get a response at first, switch to another mode. If the auditory does not work, try the kinesthetic: "How does this *feel* to you?" or "Let's *touch base* so we can get a *firm grasp* on the project."

Often, what's important is not so much the content of what you present, but the language you use to convey it—not what you communicate, but *how* you communicate it. Mirroring with words is an important way to establish the instant rapport you need to maximize your influence.

Leading the Way

Once you and another person are in synch, that person is likely to follow you. When this role reversal occurs, you know you have gained rapport. Then you can start to use that rapport to achieve the results you want. This step is called *leading*.

Remember, pacing is simply doing something similar to the other person in any of the ways discussed: matching breathing and voice, and mirroring gestures, voice tone, posture, and language style. Leading is doing something *different* from the other person and having that person match and mirror you.

If you have been successful in establishing rapport, the other person will follow your lead when you do something different from the mirroring gesture. The other person "tells" you this, but only in a nonverbal way.

Then you can send up a trial balloon (in selling, it is called a trial close) to see if the other person seems willing to accept your idea or proposal.

If the other person is not following your lead, then go back to pacing. This process of matching, pacing, and leading is a continuous one. Mirror the person's posture for a while and then change position slightly and notice whether the person follows your lead. Then you can continue mirroring and leading.

Regardless of the subject matter or form with which you intend to match, mirror, or pace and lead, the principle is always the same:

- Join people where they are
- Establish rapport

Applying Rapport Skills to Exert Influence

Rapport is defined as being "in harmony" with others. But what is required to take that rapport and apply it to influencing someone to your way of thinking? The answer can be found in a formula. The amount of influence you exercise is in direct proportion to how closely you pay attention and how flexible you are.

Influence = Attentiveness + Flexibility

Attentiveness is the ability to read another person, situation, and underlying clues. It is a human sonar system—a sensitivity to both verbal and nonverbal communication. In other words, influence depends on becoming a master practitioner of refined listening and observing—of building rapport.

Flexibility is the ability to shift to an appropriate behavior, depending on how attentive you are to the verbal and nonverbal clues the other person is giving you. You can think of flexibility this way: If you notice that what you are doing is not giving you the results you want, do not continue those same behaviors harder or longer. Instead, stop and try another tack. Almost anything else will work better than what you are already doing. You have to learn to alter your strategies to the situation and the other person to have more influence.

If you can sense important clues by being attentive and can interpret those clues as a signal to change your behavior, then you will have a better chance of getting what you want. If you have more options and choices in your responses and behaviors, you have more chances of creating a successful communication outcome.

At first, it will be trial and error until you learn what techniques work best in different situations and with different people. But as you practice, you will soon find that flexibility comes more naturally to you. Flexibility is the key to rapport and influence, and is well worth practicing.

Be attentive to what others are telling you, and be flexible enough to apply what they have told you. Remember: *Influence = Attentiveness + Flexibility*. The more attentive you are in recognizing another person's style, and the more flexible you are in dealing with that person, then the more influence you will be able to exert.

Lessening Resistance with Accommodation

Sometimes the need to be flexible in influencing another person calls for you to reconcile your motives with those of another person. But why be accommodating when you are trying to get people to think or do things your way?

Accommodation can be a key factor in softening people's resistance. A study of negotiations found that the most successful bargaining sessions occur when one party offers a few concessions (accommodations) early in the game. By offering concessions, people change the environment and are able to get more of what they wanted in the long run.

What this means is that sometimes we have to give up "being right" in the service of "winning." If you argue or try to talk people out of their needs and wants, you may score a point here or there, but you will probably not gain much in trust. Nor will you make much progress in building a strong long-term relationship.

This does not mean you should approach a negotiation as though you are giving up everything you want. What is important is an *attitude* of willingness to consider the other person's point of view and a willingness to make a few concessions if necessary. In this way you can best achieve your ultimate goals.

Accommodation Quick-Check

How accommodating are you? The qualities listed below are characteristic of those willing to accommodate others in getting what they want. Place a check (✔) by the items that apply to you:

- ❑ I am interested in the other person's needs
- ❑ A win-win situation is my preferred outcome
- ❑ I am a good listener
- ❑ I am willing to give up something to get something
- ❑ I know what I want to accomplish

Creating a Win-Win Strategy with Dovetailing

Influencing others is a positive process. You get the results you want while allowing others to get the results they want. It is a mutually beneficial relationship. Your needs and outcomes dovetail with those of the other person.

Acting without regard for other people's goals is manipulation. It is distinctly different from the interpersonal dovetailing of influence.

Dovetailing enables you to keep your own integrity while respecting the other person's integrity. Although you cannot set other people's goals for them, you can help them get what they want while you are getting what you want.

Dovetailing is key to understanding positive influence. Other people become your allies rather than your saboteurs. If people can benefit from their relationship with you, they will be more likely to help you achieve your goals. This is the most important feature of influence skills—your ability to create a win-win situation.

Tuning in to Others and Yourself

One of the most important influence skills is the ability to understand the true motives and desires of others regardless of what is being said or done on the surface. This does not mean you should not trust uneasy feelings you get in communications with others. Such feelings often signal manipulation attempts. But the most skilled communicators—those who are able to build rapport and influence others—are able to understand and empathize with others, whether the others' underlying motives are positive or negative. Skilled influencers are simply tuned in—another sign of attentiveness.

Skilled influencers also have a great deal of self-understanding. They know what their own goals are, they know what they are aiming for, and they are aware of their own strategies. Skilled influencers combine empathy and self-understanding with two other important elements: self-confidence and a desire for authority. The result is being able to reconcile your motives with those of others (*accommodation*) to meet deadlines or to move toward a solution to problems, whether those problems are obvious and stated or subtle and unspoken.

There are no shortcuts in influence. You will recognize shortcuts because they create undue pressure. But it is not necessary to induce pressure if influence skills are used effectively.

Summary

Influence = Attentiveness + Flexibility

People in general will be far more likely to respond to your communication when you work with good rapport. Therefore, you must be attentive to all their individual behaviors, from the way they breathe to the way they speak, learn, and process information. You must watch and mirror these behaviors in a natural, subtle way. Your flexibility enables you to take the lead.

By establishing good rapport on a variety of levels and speaking the same "language" as those with whom you are communicating, you are in the best position to get others to respond favorably to your ideas—whether you have direct control over them or not—and thus to achieve your goals.

Now you are a more tuned-in listener, a more aware and awake communicator, a more strategic rapport-builder. You are in charge now, with attentiveness, flexibility, and rapport coming together to make a more powerful you.

If you keep practicing these simple ideas on a daily basis, you will certainly enhance your chances to fulfill your every dream and goal.

APPENDIX

Appendix to Part 3

Comments & Suggested Responses

Break Through the Generalities

1. **"Let's work out the agenda.**

   a. Blockbusting question: What specifically do you mean by agenda?

   b. Revised statement: The list of events for the meeting.

   a. Blockbusting question: What events?

   b. Revised statement: The stress management workshops.

   a. Blockbusting question: Which workshops?

   b. Revised statement: The ones in the afternoons.

2. **"I want to get that out today."**

   a. Blockbusting question: What do you mean by "that"?

   b. Revised statement: The production reports.

   a. Blockbusting question: Which productions reports?

   b. Revised Statement: The ones for the last two quarters.

3. **"Training should cover most of the policy procedures."**

   a. Blockbusting question: Which procedures?

   b. Revised statement: The safety procedures.

   a. Blockbusting question: What kind of training do you mean?

   b. Revised Statement: CPR training.

   a. Blockbusting question: What other training?

   b. Revised statement: Specifically, CPR and lifeguard training.

4. "Higher visibility will get us the notice we want."

a. Blockbusting question: What do you mean by "higher visibility"?

b. Revised statement: More publicity.

a. Blockbusting question: What kind of publicity—local or national, broadcast, print or Internet?

b. Revised statement: We should get exposure on TV and radio.

a. Blockbusting question: What is the specific schedule you have in mind?

b. Revised statement: We should have 30 second spots on radio station WBTZ twice a week—Tues and Thurs. at drive times.

5. "We need to plan for anticipated growth."

a. Blockbusting question: What kind of planning is needed?

b. Revised statement: We should have a summary of our past growth an projections for the next few years.

a. Blockbusting question: What do you mean "few years"? How many?

b. Revised statement: Let's say three years and five years.

a. Blockbusting question: What do you mean by "growth"?

b. Revised statement: Increased production (number of units finished) and profits (22% over last year).

Clarifying Comparators

1. *That's a better way to do it.*

a. Qualifier: Better than what?

b. Qualifier: What do you mean by better?

2. *We've had very good profits this year.*

a. Qualifier: What do you mean by good?

b. Qualifier: What do you mean by "very good"?

3. *I have a better idea.*

a. Qualifier: What specifically do you mean by "better"?

b. Qualifier: Better than what?

4. *Doing it this way requires less effort.*

a. Qualifier: Less effort than what?

b. Qualifier: Doing it which way?

5. *We should set higher standards.*

a. Qualifier: Higher than what?

b. Qualifier: What standards are you referring to?

From Universal to Specific

1. **Each supervisor is responsible for her entire department.**
    a. Qualifier: The entire department?
    b. More accurate revision: All the supervisory and hourly staff.

2. **All management is concerned with is profits.**
    a. Qualifier: Profits are the only thing?
    b. More accurate revision: Management's main concern is profits.

3. **Everyone here supports the idea.**
    a. Qualifier: Everyone?
    b. More accurate revision: All but two employees support the idea.

4. **My supervisor never notices the extra work I do.**
    a. Qualifier: Never?
    b. More accurate revision: When I work late at night, my supervisor isn't there.

5. **Nobody shows me any respect.**
    a. Qualifier: Nobody?
    b. More accurate revision: My two co-workers, Joe and Dawn, don't show me respect.

6. **Everyone does the easiest thing.**
    a. Qualifier: Everyone?
    b. More accurate revision: Several people in the department take the easy way out.

7. **No one can do my job but me.**
   a. Qualifier: No one?
   b. More accurate revision: Only people with an engineering degree can do my job.

8. **My manager doesn't trust anyone.**
   a. Qualifier: No one?
   b. More accurate revision: He only trusts his relatives.

9. **I can tell you every response she'll make.**
   a. Qualifier: Every response?
   b. More accurate revision: Most of the time I can predict her response.

10. **We can't ever get what we need from the support staff.**
    a. Qualifier: Never?
    b. More accurate revision: When we ask the support staff to work late, they say no.

Additional Reading

Grinder, John and Richard Bandler. *The Structure of Magic*. Palo Alto, CA: Science & Behavior Books, 1980.

Hamlin, Sonya. *How to Talk So People Listen*. NY: Harper & Row, 1988.

Laborde, Genie Z. *Influencing with Integrity*. Palo Alto, CA: Science & Behavior Books, 1984.

McMaster, Michael and John Grinder. *Precision*. Beverly Hills, CA: Precision Models, 1980.

Richardson, Jerry. *The Magic of Rapport*, Revised Edition. Cupertino, CA: Meta Publications, 2000.

Rogers, Carl. *On Becoming a Person*. Boston, MA: Mariner Books, 1995.

Zuker, Elaina. *The Seven Secrets of Influence*. NY: McGraw-Hill, Inc., 1991.